MW01120079

World Musicmakers

Elton John

John O'Mahony

BLACKBIRCH™
PRESS

THOMSON

GALE

San Diego • Detroit • New York • San Francisco • Cleveland
New Haven, Conn. • Waterville, Maine • London • Munich

THOMSON
★
GALE

For more information, contact
The Gale Group, Inc.
27500 Drake Rd.
Farmington Hills, MI 48331-3535
Or you can visit our Internet site at http://www.gale.com

Every effort has been made to trace the owners of copyrighted material.

Photo Credits: AKG: 19; Camera Press: 13, 25, 27 (both), 28, 29, 35; Exley Publications Ltd.: 43; Gamma Press: 23, 48 (top); John Hillelson: 47; Image Select Int.: 8; London Features Int.: 6, 18, 40; Pictorial Press: 4–5, 16, 37 (left), 55, 59; Popperfoto: 7, 9; Redferns: 22, 26, 36 (top left and right), 37 (right), 39, 53; Rex Features: 15, 30, 31, 33 (top), 36 (bottom), 41 (both), 45, 46, 48 (bottom), 49, 51 (both), 54 (both), 56, 57, 58 (both); Telegraph Colour Library: 12, 38; Arnold Tendler: 10; Copyright 1975 Time Inc. Reprinted by permission: 33 (bottom).

Extracts from *Elton John* by Chris Charlesworth used by permission of Bobcat Books, a division of Book Sales Limited, 8/9 Frith Street, London W1V 5TZ.

LIBRARY OF CONGRESS CATALOGING-IN-PUBLICATION DATA

O'Mahony, John.
  Elton John / by John O'Mahony.
      p. cm. — (World musicmakers series)
  Includes index.
  Summary: Reviews the life and work of legendary rock musician Elton John, from his childhood in a quiet London suburb to superstardom and its impact on his personal life.
  ISBN 1-56711-972-7 (hardback : alk. paper)
  1. John, Elton—Juvenile literature. 2. Rock musicians—England—Biography—Juvenile literature. [1. John, Elton. 2. Musicians. 3. Rock music.] I. Title. II. Series.

  ML3930.J58O5 2004
  782.42166'092--dc21
                                                                    2003005119

Contents

Enter, stage left

On June 27, 1967, a performer named Reginald Dwight shuffled into the offices of Liberty Records on London's Regent Street. As Elton John, this young man would become famous for his musical talent and for the most extravagant stage entrances in the music business. His adopted name would dominate the charts on both sides of the Atlantic for more than two decades. He would release more than fifty singles and thirty albums, twenty-four of which would go platinum, with

Above: Reggie Dwight grew up listening to the popular music of the 1950s, including songs by Dean Martin.

Previous Page: Using the stage name Elton John, Reginald Dwight became one of the most outrageous and successful popular musicians in history.

sales of more than three hundred thousand copies. This would earn him a personal fortune of millions. One day, Elton John would account for a staggering 3 percent of total record sales, which would make him the most successful pop performer in the world.

At the age of twenty, however, Reggie Dwight was shy, a little overweight and had hair that was just beginning to thin on top. On that June day, he carried under his arm a single carrier bag crammed full of sheet music. He was invited to sit down in front of a piano. The record executive had just one thought in his head: Whatever talents might be hidden inside his chubby frame, Reggie Dwight was not conventional pop star material.

A tiny "Talent Wanted" advertisement in the music newspaper, the *New Musical Express*, had attracted Dwight's attention. He had been on a break from touring with his band, Bluesology. The ad was a ray of hope. Bluesology seemed unlikely to go anywhere. Dwight felt like a virtual prisoner behind the orange organ he played, and, vocally, he had to be content with the occasional background "Ooo" or "Aaah." He summed up his position in just three words, "I feel lost."

A good afternoon's work

It was only when Reggie Dwight flexed his fingers and launched into his first song that there was even a hint of the performer who would one day cast his boisterous, sequined shadow over the piano keys. Dwight definitely had something.

Even then, his voice had a plaintive quality that was good for romantic, sentimental ballads such as "Candle in the Wind" and "Your Song." Dwight also wrote his own material, although, in his own estimation, he was "no good" at writing lyrics. The record executive hastily arranged a meeting with someone who could write lyrics: Bernie Taupin. Taupin had sent in a few obscure, dog-eared lyric sheets in response to the same advertisement. Little did anyone know that, over the course of one short afternoon, one of the greatest songwriting duos in the history of pop music would come together.

The beginning

On March 25, 1947, Pinner, a quiet London suburb, became the birthplace of Reggie Dwight. Reggie's father, Stanley Dwight, had joined the Royal Air Force (RAF) during World War II. He began to date a nineteen-year-old clerk, Sheila Harris. They were married in 1945 and settled down at 55 Pinner Hill Road. After the war, Stanley stayed on in the RAF and was soon promoted to the rank of flight lieutenant. This meant he had to spend long stretches away from home. During those times, mother and son enjoyed the music of the day together: Nat King Cole, Dean Martin, Guy Mitchell, and Rosemary Clooney.

When he was on leave, however, Stanley ran the Dwight family home like an RAF barracks. "He never let me do anything that I wanted," Reggie Dwight remembered. "I couldn't even play in the garden in case I might damage his rose beds."

Both Sheila and her son began to dread the moment when the flight lieutenant came home. Reggie later described his feelings as a terrible inferiority complex. Only the fact that his mother defended him when his parents argued prevented his feelings of inferiority from overwhelming him.

Despite their poor relationship, it was from his father, Stanley, who played the trumpet, that Reggie inherited his musical talent. "When I was seven my dad gave me a copy of Frank Sinatra's 'Songs for Swinging Lovers' which wasn't really the ideal present for a seven-year-old. I really wanted a bicycle." Reggie's natural aptitude for music showed when he was just a child. His grandmother often sat him at the piano to keep him amused, and she found that, even as a five-year-old, he could play entire songs.

Rock and roll

At school, Reggie was a quiet, orderly, and well-behaved boy. He was also shy and reserved and sometimes became a target of bullies. It did not help matters that from a very young age, Reggie had a weight problem.

There was one thing that Reggie did very well, but he did not flaunt his talent. He excelled at music and at a very

Pianist and singer Nat King Cole was one of Reginald Dwight's earliest musical influences.

young age, completed grade eight, the top grade, on the piano at London's prestigious Royal Academy. Soon, he had begun to give spirited performances of "Hound Dog" by Elvis Presley, "Rock Around the Clock" by Bill Haley and the Comets, and "Good Golly Miss Molly" by Jerry Lee Lewis. Also on his playlist was Little Richard. All of these songs made him very popular among his classmates.

His Royal Academy training gave Reggie a solid background. For the grade eight exam, he had to play complicated scales. He also had to play classical pieces of music, such as Beethoven's "Sonata in F Minor" or Chopin's "Polonaise in C# Minor." Although Reggie never spent hours deliberating over a particular note or musical phrase, his skill and knowledge of technique combined with his natural talent allowed him to work at a dazzling speed. He recalled, "I thought my formal education was a drag at the time. I really didn't want to learn the piano properly. I was quite happy playing in C or G which are the easiest keys to play in as a keyboard player. But looking back, it did me a lot of good to learn chord structures and other keys."

Reggie Dwight grew up in this suburban London house at 55 Pinner Hill Road.

Reggie Dwight's cousin, Roy Dwight (number 6), was a famous soccer player.

Second only to young Reggie's enthusiasm for music was his love of soccer. His attempts to play on the soccer field always ended in frustration, however. It did not seem likely that Reggie would ever realize his dream of taking part in professional soccer.

Professional already?

When Reggie was fifteen, his parents decided to get a divorce. It was a very painful time for the young man. He rarely wanted to talk about his home situation. Stanley named Sheila's friendship with painter and decorator Fred Farebrother as the reason for the divorce.

Although the divorce saddened him, life at home did become easier for Reggie. Fred Farebrother's presence at the dinner table delighted him, and one change overshadowed all others. Fred Farebrother began to take an active interest in Reggie's musical career.

In retrospect, there were certainly many better places to start as a professional musician than the Northwood Hills

Hotel in Pinner. Few of them, however, would have been willing to take on a shy pianist in a tweed jacket and flannels. Even more bizarre were the young boy's glasses, which he wore as a tribute to his hero, Buddy Holly. Reggie wore them all the time, even though he did not really need them.

Fred Farebrother organized an audition at the hotel, and soon, Reggie was playing "When Irish Eyes Are Smiling" and "Bye Bye Blackbird" to an audience made up mainly of couples and drunken old men. At first, the crowd did not take to the new entertainer. They shouted, "Get off!" and dumped the contents of their ashtrays on the future superstar.

Singing the blues

Reggie, now sixteen, had also formed a band with friends Stuart Brown and Geoff Dyson and a boy with the unusual name of Elton Dean. Called Bluesology, they played music inspired by the soul sounds of American record companies such as Motown and Stax. It was pop music with an African-American blues and jazz feel—lots of syncopated rhythm that hit the normally unaccented beats.

With his friends, Reggie Dwight (far right) formed the band Bluesology in 1963.

Bluesology was very much a formula band of the period. The members all dressed in similar uniforms, including turtleneck sweaters, in the style the Beatles had set. Reggie played an electric organ, which he had managed to buy with money saved from his Northwood Hills job, and he traded off with the charismatic Stu Brown as lead vocalist.

Reggie was not satisfied with such marginal musical involvement, though, especially since Stu Brown seemed determined to monopolize the spotlight. Fred Farebrother had helped Reggie take the first step to a life in the music business. His second step, taken almost entirely alone, caused outrage, but it was one that he felt sure of. As he put it: "I had to be involved in music."

At the age of seventeen, not long before his exams were due to begin, Reggie Dwight left school. He had found a job as a message boy with a music publisher in London's West End. On his last day at school, one of the teachers remarked, "When you're forty, you may end up as a glorified office boy . . . or a millionaire."

First push

Life in the music business was far from wonderful. Most of the time Reggie loafed around in dingy offices. He spent nights on stage with Bluesology who, like most new bands, played venues in the hope that they would be noticed by a record company. Bluesology proved to be among the lucky ones. They managed to secure a recording contract.

Their first single was called "Come Back, Baby." It was both sung and written, as the record label testifies, by R. Dwight. In November 1964, a second single, "Mr. Fantastic," was recorded for release early the next year. It, too, bore the same sleeve credit and featured the same lead vocalist. It looked like Reggie Dwight might just be a household name one day.

Second from the left at the back

Despite a few good reviews, both singles failed to make any impression. Bluesology reluctantly went back on the road. Their salary, though, was high enough to turn them all into full-time professional musicians, and they

> "When we [Bluesology] came back to England, I started getting really frustrated and complex-ridden because I was extremely large, about fourteen stone [196 pounds], and I was stuck behind a Vox Continental organ when what I really wanted to do was sing."
>
> —Elton John, from *Elton John* by Chris Charlesworth

opened for major American bands who were on tour in Great Britain.

This was little consolation to Reggie. The next year and a half was by far the most artistically frustrating of his life. Stu Brown, with his Mediterranean good looks, took over as front man of Bluesology, and a blues veteran, Long John Baldry, took control of the band. Night after night, Reggie found that he had no choice but to play someone else's songs.

When it all became too much, Reggie expressed his torment with fits of temper, or "screaming fits," as they became known. These outbursts were sometimes so severe that the other band members ran and hid when they saw one beginning. These moods were made worse by Reggie's constant dieting. He often took pills in order to keep his weight down.

Until the day when he saw that advertisement in the *New Musical Express*, Reggie Dwight was a dejected figure who felt as if he were on the fringes of his own band. He was really lost.

Year of the teddy bear

Meanwhile, seventeen-year-old Bernie Taupin spent the summer of 1967 with his nose stuck in a book. He had just discovered author J.R.R. Tolkien. During his childhood on a farm in the sedate surroundings of England's Lincolnshire, Taupin's imagination had been fed both by serious writers such as Alfred Lord Tennyson and Samuel Taylor Coleridge and by the light-heartedness of A. A. Milne's *Winnie-the-Pooh*. He was also an avid reader of Western stories about outlaws such as Jesse James and Billy the Kid.

Inspired by what he read, Taupin began to write what he considered poetry. When rock and roll entered his life, he realized that he had actually been writing song lyrics in those early years. They were perfect for the styles popularized by performers such as the Beatles and Bob Dylan.

One day, Taupin wrapped up some lyrics and sent them to an address he saw at the bottom of a small advertisement he had spotted in a corner of the *New Musical Express*. He then entirely forgot about it until he

Below and opposite: The 1960s was a decade of colorful fashion and new types of music. It was in this atmosphere that Reggie Dwight developed his own musical style and dress code.

received a letter that asked him to drop in to the music company's office if he were ever in the area of Regent Street in London. Bernie Taupin made sure that he was.

The misfits

At the recording studio, Reggie Dwight and Bernie Taupin were introduced to each other and quickly became acquainted. They shared facts and stories about Motown, the Beatles, and Bob Dylan. Taupin had expected Dwight to be a big rock star with an ego to match. Instead, he found that Dwight was a piano player of fairly small stature whose ego had been crushed by the events of the previous year. Over two cups of coffee, the pair decided to write a few songs together.

• •

". . . we [Elton John and Bernie Taupin] met and we went round the corner to the Lancaster Grill and had a couple of cups of coffee. I passed him over the state secrets [the lyrics], and that, as they say, is history."

—Bernie Taupin, from *Two Rooms*

• •

13

It could not have been more perfect: a union of mis-fits. "I remember he [Taupin] looked quite angelic," Elton John later said. "And he was very young. We got on very well. He was shy, which made two of us. I really adored him from the word go; he was like the brother I never had."

"We did find a natural affinity," remembered Bernie Taupin, "partly because we were both loners. I was a loner because I was a country boy in the big city, so I was a little out of my depth. And, although Elton had been around the block, he'd toured and he'd clubbed with major American artists and seen a lot of things, I still think that he was fairly naive."

If the arrangement did not work out, they agreed that they would simply go their separate ways. If the partnership did prove successful, anything might happen. They both agreed that neither of them had anything to lose.

Moonlighting

Bernie Taupin went back to the farm in Lincolnshire and sent any lyrics that he wrote to Reggie Dwight who, although still officially part of Bluesology, then wrote the music to go with them. The partners intended to get other musicians to perform their songs.

To succeed, this new songwriting partnership needed to make demos of its work, rough recordings made in a studio with professional equipment. These demos could then be taken to different record companies to try to generate some interest.

"We were very young," Elton John reminisced. "We went through tremendous enjoyment and tremendous hope. The tremendous hope when someone's going to do your song and you count on it and then the despair if they say no they're not going to do it. We went through incredible depressions and frustrations."

A friend from Dwight's message boy days allowed the pair access to a recording studio. The friend did not, however, get permission from the studio's owner, Dick James, the man who had discovered the Beatles. One night, when the studio manager drove by, he noticed that all the lights were still on. The undercover

recording session was broken up and the moonlighters were reported to Dick James.

If Dwight and Taupin wanted to use his studio to record their music, Dick James insisted, they should at least allow him to hear it. James liked what he heard. The two were signed up with Dick James Music for $40 a week. They had become professional songwriters.

They were also earning what they considered to be a fortune. The money allowed Dwight to indulge one of his vices: binge buying, particularly records, which he had collected avidly since his teenage years. Dwight often visited bargain record stores and bought as many records as he could carry.

Partnership

With financial independence, Bernie Taupin was able to move to London, and Reggie Dwight was able to leave Bluesology. They moved into a basement apartment together. Everything did not work out as they had planned, though.

Reggie Dwight had a close musical partnership with Bernie Taupin (right), who wrote the lyrics to most of Dwight's songs.

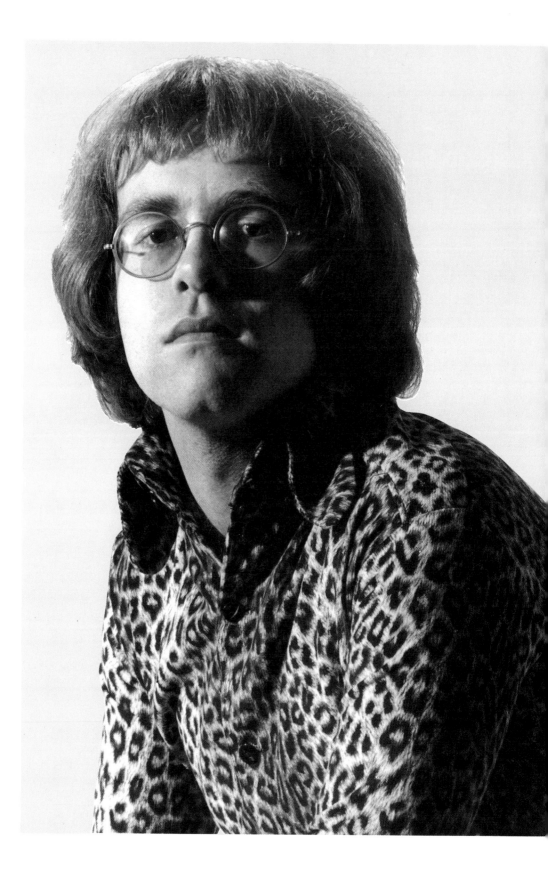

Reggie Dwight was engaged to a girl he knew from his Bluesology days, Linda Woodrow. They were not a very compatible couple, though. Often, Dwight and Taupin's work was interrupted by Dwight's violent arguments with Woodrow. The situation reached a climax when Dwight tried unsuccessfully to commit suicide. After this, Dwight broke off the engagement. Taupin and Dwight then moved in with Dwight's mother and Fred Farebrother the next day. They stayed there for a year and a half.

In the Farebrother household, Dwight and Taupin lived like schoolboys. They shared a room, slept in bunkbeds, and spent all their time together. They also formulated the songwriting system that they used throughout their long career.

The process was made up of two entirely separate phases. First, Bernie Taupin wrote the lyrics as he sat in the top bunk. When he had finished, he handed the sheet over to Dwight who took a brief look at it. Then, Dwight rushed to the piano and wrote music for the song.

Unique technique

Sometimes, the duo could compose a piece of music in minutes. "They were very naive lyrics and they were very naive melodies," said Dwight, "but there was a chemistry there and I enjoyed doing it." Like most pop lyrics, Taupin's compositions contained a number of conventional elements that give a song a recognizable structure. First, there is the chorus, also known as the refrain. It is made up of a series of repeated phrases, and it introduces the song's central theme. Often the chorus is also the title of the song. In Bernie Taupin's songs, this pattern is best demonstrated in "The Bitch Is Back," a song in which the title is repeated more than forty times in just four minutes.

The chorus also usually uses the best part of the melody, or tune. This is called the hook, because, as the name implies, it enters the listener's memory and stays there. In "Candle in the Wind," Dwight used a soaring, instantly recognizable melody for his hook.

For the rest of a composition, the melody is more reserved so that the hook stands out. Dwight's melodies

. . . .

"Elton relied more on the sound of words than their literal meaning. His major talent, apart from a limitless ability to write catchy hook lines, was in his pronunciation and phrasing of Taupin's lyrics. This dramatic style of delivery made them seem significant, squeezed emotion from the nonsense, and made the words more memorable still."

—Chris Charlesworth,
from *Elton John*

. . . .

In the late 1960s, Reggie Dwight took the stage name Elton John, a combination of two friends' names.

17

Bernie Taupin and Reggie Dwight's songwriting method was unique among their peers.

are deceptively simple, however. The main rhythm of the melody is straightforward. Underneath, though, the chord pattern, in which three or more notes are played at the same time, is often quite complex.

The method of composition that Bernie Taupin and Reggie Dwight established is unique among songwriters and performers. Most other partners usually work in unison on both the lyrics and music, and each collaborator makes suggestions as the song takes shape.

It never occurred to Dwight and Taupin to work this way, however. The only time they got together was to hear the opinion of Dwight's mother, Sheila Farebrother, who judged the duo's work. She explained, "They used to wait for me at the window and as soon as I got in it was: 'Come and listen to this.' If it was one I cried at, they'd say: 'Well that's a winner, we'll have that one.'"

Formula for success

Reggie Dwight and Bernie Taupin had worked out a formula to create the perfect pop song. "We're not really the public's idea of a songwriting team, you know, two guys sweating over a hot piano, shirtsleeves rolled up, shades on," they admitted. "We're very unprofessional." Their work became a model for a whole generation of songwriters. The lyrics of their songs are full of images but are simple enough not to make the songs too complex. Pop lyrics call for a delicate balance. If the words are too poetic, they will be in competition with the music. On the other hand, if the lyrics are too simple or bland, the song will be boring. Individuality, Bernie Taupin explained, is the key. "I certainly never try to write a conventional love song. . . . Who wants to hear a happy love song? Love songs should be all about broken hearts and darkness and sadness. Songs are about people listening to them and relating to them." Lyrics also need to be full of images that can inspire the composer of the music as well as the listener. "One of the nicest compliments I'm often paid is that the content of our songs is very cinematic," Taupin said.

Sometimes, however, Reggie Dwight did not know what Taupin's lyrics were about, and he cut out verses. He said, "I don't understand some of the lyrics, especially the earlier ones: 'Take Me to the Pilot.' I've no idea what that's about. Nor does Bernie."

The wordsmith

The pair's vast collection of songs offers many examples of their songwriting technique. Their song "Daniel," for example, tells the story of a Vietnam War soldier who is leaving his hometown. When he returns after the war, his old friends do not know how to treat him. They regard him as either a hero or a freak. He just wants his old life back. When Dwight wrote the music to accompany Taupin's lyrics, however, he cut the final verse, which gave most of those details.

Instead, Daniel's story is told with a haunting, wrenching melody. It means many things to each listener, but it always imparts a feeling of tragedy and loss. "Daniel is travelling tonight on a plane. I can see

Bernie Taupin's words and Reggie Dwight's music created many memorable songs, including "Candle in the Wind," a tribute to Marilyn Monroe.

the red tail lights, heading for Spain. Oh and I can see Daniel waving goodbye. God, it looks like Daniel, must be the clouds in my eyes."

Other penetrating lyrics that Dwight combined with a plaintive melody and memorable, sorrowful hook, can be found in "Candle in the Wind," a lament for Marilyn Monroe, who changed her name from Norma Jean Baker as she rose to stardom. The lyrics ran: "And it seems to me you lived your life like a candle in the wind. Never knowing who to cling to when the rain set in. And I would have liked to have known you, but I was just a kid. Your candle burned out long before your legend ever did."

The birth of Elton John

As the Reggie Dwight and Bernie Taupin duo gradually built up their repertoire of songs, the spotlight of Dick James's attention slowly edged in their direction. The pair were trying to raise interest not only in their song-writing skills, but also in Dwight's own potential as a performer.

James agreed to release a single, but he believed no one could be a pop star with a name like Reggie Dwight. The name would have to go. "A young person's name is not Reginald," Elton John said later. "It sounded like a cement mixer. And Reggie is terrible too, a nightmare. It's not so bad in America. Like, Reggie Jackson doesn't sound so bad. But, in England, it just doesn't make it."

The single they released flopped, but it did have an important legacy. The song's failure banished Reggie Dwight forever, and it introduced Elton John. The new name was a combination of names from former Bluesology partners, Elton Dean and Long John Baldry. As the newly renamed piano player said, "Elton John was the person Reg Dwight always wanted to be."

The duo's next two singles did not fare much better with the public. They were received well by disc jockeys and the music press, however. So Dick James gave the go-ahead for the first Elton John album to be produced.

Empty Sky was a wistful, flimsy collection of John-Taupin compositions that showed the duo in a delicate, embryonic stage. It sold twenty thousand copies, which was not bad for an entirely unknown artist. "It [the album] still holds the nicest memories for me," Elton John remembers, "because it was the first, I suppose. It's difficult to explain the amazing enthusiasm we felt as the album began to take shape but I remember when we finished work on the title track it just floored me. I thought it was the best thing I'd ever heard in my life."

The 1970s

A new decade brought a whole new generation of stars. At the same time, the breakup of the Beatles in 1970 marked a great watershed in pop music.

The 1960s had been dominated by groups, whereas the early 1970s were dominated by individual performers. The 1960s had been the decade of the guitar, but the piano came to prominence in the new era. Later, the synthesizer, an instrument that could reproduce almost any known sound electronically, changed the face of live and recorded pop music.

Dick James pledged thousands of dollars and fifty-five hours of recording time to Elton John's second album. This huge amount of money allowed John and Taupin to acquire the services of David Bowie's *Space Oddity* album producer, Gus Dudgeon, whose role was to control the overall sound of the record and its musical direction. John also used the services of Bowie's arranger, Paul Buckmaster, to create the musical accompaniment of the full orchestra they needed. Elton John was splashing into the 1970s.

A hit at last

The new album, entitled *Elton John*, presented its title performer with a fuller, rounder sound. It contained a mix of songs that were lyrically and musically well crafted. One, "Your Song," is something that Elton John and Bernie Taupin rarely matched in the future. Its lyrics read: "And you can tell everybody, this is your song. It may be quite simple but, now that it's done, I hope you don't mind, I hope you don't mind that I put down in words how wonderful life is while you're in the world."

The album began to invade British airwaves and was championed by a number of disc jockeys. It made it to

....

"Elton is everything. Elton's the consummate performer, the consummate musician. Elton rocks, Elton's soft, Elton plays the best rock 'n' roll piano ever and he can deliver a ballad better than anybody I know, he enjoys it, and that's why he's so good at it."

—Bernie Taupin, from *Two Rooms*

....

21

number eleven on the British charts and ranked along-side "Let It Be" by the Beatles and "Bridge over Troubled Water" by Simon and Garfunkel.

At the same time, twenty-three-year-old Elton John tentatively began to attempt live performances. He was painfully shy. At first, he showed no more charisma than he had on that day when he walked into the Liberty office. His confidence grew as his waistline shrank, however. During a concert at London's Roundhouse, Elton John kicked away the piano stool and performed a piano handstand, a flamboyant stage gesture that became his trademark.

"Madman Across the Water"

Now convinced that John was a quality artist, Dick James was eager to introduce the performer to American audiences. James sanctioned a small promotional tour. The highlight of the tour was to be a showcase evening at the Los Angeles Troubadour Club in front of an invited audience of media and music business guests.

Above: Although he was a shy young man, Elton John was confident on stage.

Opposite: Elton John's piano handstand became a highlight of his shows.

23

As the evening of the show approached, Elton John became more and more nervous. He sulked and let himself fall into a state of absolute terror. Soon, his entourage began to see what the members of Bluesology had come to know very well. "Elton was starting to get a bit desperate," remembered Dick James's son, Steve, "and I would say his tantrums began to manifest themselves around this time because he wanted to make sure everything was done to insure the product was successful."

Just before the show was about to start, John was ready to cancel. His manager had left him completely alone at this nerve-wracking moment, and when the manager finally returned, he noticed that "Elton was very weird. I realized that being left alone all day had put him in some kind of bad mental state." Only after some frantic late-night phone calls to Dick James in London was John able to calm himself down.

A gallery of stars gathered inside the Troubadour Club on August 25, 1970. They had all been enticed to come by the prospect of a free evening. They certainly had not come to see the performance on stage. Elton John may have been a promising newcomer, but most of the people there that night had never heard of him.

During John's first few songs, his singing could barely be heard above the general chatter. Nobody was paying attention. By his third number, he had begun to frown. Then, he began to get angry. Finally, he jumped up and shouted, "If you don't like what I'm playing, maybe it's a little rock 'n' roll that you want." Then, he launched into his next song with gusto. From that moment, on the audience was captivated.

Explosion

The following day, the reviewers were ecstatic. Overnight, Elton John had been transformed into a star.

Within only two weeks of the Troubadour opening, the *Elton John* album had sold thirty-thousand copies across America. The reviewers competed with each other to praise the new star. The tour that had once been intended only to test the water had opened the floodgates. The *Chicago Sun-Times* had discovered "a

"People who have hit records come and go, but you can't sustain a career unless you play live. And I don't mean just lipsynching or playing to a drum track because that's not playing live. A lot of artists go out there and do that nowadays and that's why they have the charisma of a dead pea."

—Elton John, from *Two Rooms*

major star by the end of the first set." A Hollywood reporter found the act "spectacularly exciting." It was Robert Hilburn at the *Los Angeles Times*, however, who proved to be the real star-maker. "By the end of the evening there was no question about John's talent and potential," he wrote. "Tuesday night at the Troubadour was just the beginning. He's going to be one of rock's biggest and most important stars."

As a superstar musician, Elton John dressed and acted outrageously for his performances. In a 1975 performance at Dodger Stadium in Los Angeles, California, he wore a sequined baseball uniform

Neither Elton John nor the band really understood exactly what was happening. The tour was immediately extended to include dates in Philadelphia and New York. No one along the way was about to contradict Hilburn's opinion: Elton John was "the first rock superstar of the 1970s."

It quickly became obvious that Elton John's performing persona was changing. The shy introvert had begun to disappear. At every concert, John shed a skin, and each new layer was more flamboyant and more outrageous than the previous one. At a show in Santa Monica, California, for example, he wore a leather top hat, a sky-blue velvet cloak, and thigh-high silver boots encrusted with stars. His face was almost hidden by enormous glasses.

Back in Great Britain, news of the transformation had begun to spread. "I remember when these pictures started to arrive of him on tour in the States," recalled Dick James employee Sue Ayton. "Everyone back in the office said 'What on earth is going on?' But Steve Brown [the publicity manager] said, 'No this is great, this is the way it is going to be.'"

Each of Elton John's stage outfits was complemented by a matching set of antics. He sometimes flicked away the piano stool during a number, did handstands on the keyboard, or played on his knees like Jerry Lee Lewis.

Confirmation of Elton John's American star status came at the end of 1971 when he was named top male vocalist by *Record World* magazine. Elton John and Bernie Taupin were also named as best composers of the year. It soon became clear that even without a hit single, the traditional gateway to popularity with the record-buying public, Elton John was one of the greatest performers of all time.

Composing over breakfast

Then, "Your Song" was released. The simple, direct love song with its sorrowful melody was not an obvious choice for a hit. Dick James had doubted whether it was wise to release it. It turned out to be the right decision, however. It gave Elton John his first hit in Great Britain, though it did not reach number one on the charts. Even

This page and opposite: Elton John became known for his outrageous fashions and wild eyeglasses.

27

Elton John managed his own career for roughly a year until he met record label manager, John Reid.

so, the level of success was impressive for a song that had been composed over breakfast at John's mother's house.

"Your Song" earned praise from some very renowned celebrities. "There was something about his vocals," commented John Lennon, "that was an improvement on all the English vocals till then. When I heard it I thought 'Great! That's the first thing that's happened since we [the Beatles] happened.'"

The quiet man

In January 1971, at the age of twenty-three, Elton John set off for a festival in the south of France to attempt to launch his career in Europe. Then, he briefly toured Scandinavia. For most of the rest of that year, he made his way across North America.

John himself gradually turned into a one-man rock-and-roll circus. During concerts, Bernie Taupin watched from the side of the stage and waited for the moment when his partner called him out from the wings and introduced him as the lyricist of the songs John had performed. Then, Taupin shuffled out in front of the crowd, waved a little, and returned to the sidelines.

A new manager

As far as management was concerned, Elton John had been drifting haphazardly since his Troubadour days a year before. Soon after that performance, John's manager had been fired. Afterward, John had no real management until a young record label manager named John Reid arrived on the scene.

Reid was a tough Scotsman from a rough area of Glasgow. Soon, Elton John's interests became Reid's own. John Reid had a profound influence on the star's career both as manager and friend.

Sprees, houses, and general spending

Elton John had always been an avid record collector. Now that he had increased his bank balance considerably, he could buy records every day if he wished. His shopping sprees became legendary.

Elton John became known for spending a lot of money. Here, he poses in front of his custom-built luxury airliner, Starship I.

Above: One of Elton John's many houses featured this elaborate garden.

Middle and below: Elton John decorated his London apartment with expensive furnishings, and memorabilia such as the oversized Doc Marten boots he wore in the film Tommy.

The urge for collecting extended far beyond records, though. In 1972, John acquired a house in Virginia Water, forty-five minutes outside of London. He called it "Hercules," which was by then his middle name.

He bought antiques, paintings, and jewelry in the same huge quantities he had previously done with records. His most notable purchase came in 1984, when he bought a streetcar in Australia for $8,993.

John also frequently gave lavish gifts to his friends. Sometimes, he gave a person a car. Other times, it

Above: Elton John retreated to this home in Saint-Tropez, France, when he needed a break from his hectic life.

might be a house or a gold Cartier watch. To his manager, John Reid, Elton John once gave a yacht worth $80,000 and a clock worth $10,000.

At this time, John's career was at its healthiest, but he was under tremendous stress. His contract with Dick James Music required him to release two albums a year. This would be unheard of in the more open-ended contracts of today.

Touring commitments were also tough. John's workload had quadrupled, and so had his temper tantrums. He sulked and needed careful handling in order to cooperate. Furthermore, by June 1972, the band was at work once again, recording John's next album, *Don't Shoot Me, I'm Only the Piano Player.*

The strain was just too much. With his natural ear for music, Elton John could quickly compose a melody to go with any set of lyrics. He had written twelve new songs in just two days. The amount of work brought him close to a nervous breakdown, though. "I was never worried from a musical point of view. But personality-wise, I had become unbearable," he commented shortly after. His Italian tour was stopped, and twenty-six-year-old Elton John took a much-deserved rest. At the end of the year, he was well enough to make an extensive three-month tour of the United States.

The battle over "Daniel"

The choice of an advance single to accompany the release of *Don't Shoot Me* in 1973 turned out to be a bigger problem than Elton John or Bernie Taupin could have imagined. Dick James felt that the upbeat "Crocodile Rock" was the obvious choice. The songwriting duo, however, preferred the unusual downbeat ballad "Daniel." In accord with James's choice, "Crocodile Rock" was released.

Even after "Crocodile Rock" reached number one in the United States, however, John Elton still wanted "Daniel" to be released as a single. When Dick James refused, John lashed out at his own record company from the pages of the music press. "It's one of the best songs I've ever written," he said. "I don't care if it's a hit or not. I want it out."

In the end, Dick James relented. He chose, though, not to pay for publicity unless the record made it into the Top 10, and he felt the chances of that were minimal. Contrary to his predictions, "Daniel" was a huge success. It went to number two in the United States and number four in Great Britain. Elton John's stardom reached new heights. Crowds of girls began to chase him into hotels, and audiences screamed at concerts. *Don't Shoot Me* went to number one in both the United States and Great Britain at the same time, John's first album to do so.

Following the disagreement about the release of "Daniel," Elton John was determined to do something to allow recording artists more say and to give them a fairer deal with record bosses. The catalyst came when the guitarist of Elton John's band, Davey Johnson, wanted to record his own album. Despite help from both Elton John and John Reid, Johnson found it impossible to find a suitable record label. "We just got very drunk one night and said that we would start our own label," Elton John confessed at the time. As a result, Rocket Records came into being. It offered its clients good terms, and most importantly, "undivided love and attention."

John wanted the new label to help struggling performers more than he wanted to use it to promote his own career. He was still contracted to Dick James Music anyway. "We just want to be a friendly record company," John said. The label closed down for new artists in 1987; Elton John remained the label's only act.

More extravagance

Elton John's legendary stage show had reached maturity by the time he embarked on the Yellow Brick Road tour in 1973. The name of the tour came from the double album he released that year. At the Hollywood Bowl, John made his entrance dressed all in white feathers, from a modestly sized cap to a large pair of pants. As he arrived, five piano lids opened, each spelling out a letter of his name, and four hundred white doves flew up from behind the stage. Later on, he changed into a purple jumpsuit and a pair of glasses that lit up like headlights.

Elton John's trademark glasses inspired fans (above) and were a vital part of his image (below).

John's career went through many style changes. Over the years, he dressed as Mozart, Minnie Mouse, a Russian cossack, and once, as Tina Turner in a leather miniskirt. He was rarely seen without his trademark spectacles. Some were gaudy and outrageous. Others were works of art. One pair spelled "ELTON" in giant letters across his face. The glasses were so large that, had it not been for the name, it might have been difficult to know who was underneath them. "Bernie hated some of the costumes that I wore," Elton John recalled. "[And] hated some of the things that I did. But I had to be me. I think I took it too far in retrospect, but I can't regret that now. He was embarrassed by some of it and he will admit that freely. And looking back on the photographs, I can see why."

Caribou

The year 1974 began disastrously. The album *Caribou* was put together quickly in mid-February under the least promising of circumstances.

Bernie Taupin and Elton John had little time to compose during the hectic previous year, and only ten days could be spared in John's schedule for composition, rehearsal, and recording. He had to push the pace faster than even this speedy duo could endure. "It's a miracle that the *Caribou* album came out," Elton John said. "Because of all the pressure within the group; especially with me. We'd been on the road for four-and-a-half years and we all looked like unbelievable zombies and we were just on the point of breaking up."

Around this time, John's weight ballooned, mainly because of the amount of alcohol he was consuming. In retrospect, he admitted that he was on the verge of addiction problems, some of which affected him for many years to come. He recalled, "I mean, I was just becoming an alcoholic. It was just ridiculous."

Only the location, a studio ranch high up in the Colorado mountains, seemed to offer any hope at all for *Caribou*. Breathtaking scenery alone could not save this album, however. Tempers flared as progress seemed unsatisfactory. John's temper tantrums showed a disregard for all the people working on the album. He was simply

• •

"I have the most blessed life: I go around, I sing, I stay in the most opulent places, I have an opulent lifestyle. The least I can do is to put some of my earnings back into organizations that help, that spend their lives treating people that are far less fortunate than myself."

—Elton John

• •

34

eager to get the album finished before he embarked on a tour of Japan, Australia, and New Zealand.

Charity

At this time, the early 1970s, it was unusual for stars to pledge time and support for fundraising events. Therefore, when Elton John stepped out on stage to raise money for the Invalid Children's Society, it was a groundbreaking move. John also became chairman of Watford Football Club, a soccer team in Great Britain. A concert he gave at the club's grounds raised more than $80,000.

John's example soon spread throughout the pop music establishment. Concerts to raise money for charity became very popular, especially during the 1980s.

A measure of success

At Los Angeles's Dodger Stadium, in November 1975, one hundred thousand people saw Elton John perform. The seven-day period before the concert was officially pronounced Elton John Week. During that week, John pressed his stubby fingers into the cold, sludgy concrete on Hollywood's Walk of Fame just as Marilyn Monroe, Judy Garland, and other legendary stars had done before him. He was now truly famous.

Elton John spent much of 1975 in the United States. He rented a house that was full of dark, cavernous rooms and long, shadowy corridors, not the sort of place for an exhausted pop star living miles away from home, friends, and family. As a result, his mental health began to suffer.

A friend and ex-employee of Rocket Records, Sharon Lawrence, visited Elton John during this period. "I remembered this person who was mildly temperamental," she said. "Who could be a bit neurotic and difficult, but who was basically happy and organized. Now he looked ghastly, he was incredibly strung up, anxious and panicky . . . he seemed to have become a complete wreck."

During this time, John attempted suicide on several occasions. He also began to gain weight again. He had always been a binge dieter, but his weight fluctuations

In 1975, Elton John performed for a crowd of one hundred thousand people at Dodger Stadium in Los Angeles.

Over the years, Elton John's costumes, hats, and headdresses became increasingly elaborate.

gradually grew more extreme. This led him to develop the eating disorder bulimia, in which the sufferer overeats and then vomits to prevent digestion and weight gain. The disease does extensive damage to the stomach and the teeth as vomiting brings acid from the stomach and partially digested food up to the mouth. The psychological damage is also severe.

Added to this crisis was the strain of John's 1975 work schedule. The year had seen him perform as the Pinball Wizard in the movie *Tommy*. He promoted the new album *Captain Fantastic and the Brown Dirt Cowboy*. He rehearsed feverishly for a performance before seventy-two thousand fans at Wembley Stadium in London. He recorded another album, *Rock of the Westies*, appeared at a three-night charity concert at the Los Angeles Troubadour Club, did a short tour of the United States and Canada, and gave two concerts at Dodger Stadium. By the end of the year, twenty-eight-year-old Elton John was advised by doctors to take four

"Gradually he cast all inhibitions aside and his wardrobe became more and more colorful, star-spangled boots, jump-suits and outsized hats. But most of all the impression he gave was of an artist enjoying himself in his work and communicating that enjoyment to his audience in what often seemed to be a spirit of cheerful self-mockery."

—Chris Charlesworth, from *Elton John*

During the mid-1970s, punk rock became increasingly popular and influenced fashion. Many punk rockers wore mohawk hairdos and leather clothes.

months' rest. Thus, John began the latter half of the decade in recovery in Barbados. His public profile began to wane as a result.

The rise of punk

In general, 1976 was a very quiet year for Elton John. It was a noisy one for the music industry, though, as punk rock became popular. Bands such as the Sex Pistols, the Clash, and the Damned arrived on the music scene wearing decaying leather jackets, Mohawk haircuts, and safety pins in their noses and earlobes.

The anarchic, discordant music that punk rock produced rebelled against the sweet melodies of Elton John's generation. Plumed, loud-mouthed, irreverent renegades such as Johnny Rotten, the front man of the Sex Pistols, proclaimed themselves to be the way forward. Elton John seemed part of the past.

The only release from John's album *Rock of the Westies* was "Grow Some Funk of Your Own." It peaked at a disappointing number fourteen in the United States. When a hit did materialize for Elton John, it was a song from the past. "Pinball Wizard" from *Tommy* was by then two years old.

In limbo

Bernie Taupin was, at the same time, going through a period of physical and emotional fatigue. He had been on the road with Elton John for more than five years. He had always waited patiently for his five-minute introduction and his paychecks from the 50 percent share he held in Elton John's music.

The rigorous schedule began to take a toll on Taupin, however. His private life had not been running very smoothly. His marriage of four years had broken up. He had entered into an artistic limbo and took solace in drinking and drugs.

Crisis point

In 1977, Elton John turned thirty, which can be a difficult hurdle for many people. For a pop star, youth and appearance are of paramount importance. Elton John was no longer young. His hair had been thinning for years. By now, he might officially be considered bald. For the next few years, he underwent many painful and unsuccessful attempts to have hair transplants. The transplants removed plugs, or squares, of healthy hair from one part of the scalp and sewed them on to the bald patches. John's personal assistant, Andrew Hill, remembered one incident: "As he went to get into the car, he hit his head on the top of the door, knocking half of the squares out."

Hill also recalled other times with his boss. He accompanied Elton John to numerous parties where cocaine was consumed in large quantities. Around the same time, John and Bernie Taupin met Elvis Presley, whose life was now ruled by drugs. Seeing Presley becoming a casualty of the fast life he was living, Elton John began to think about his own future and how his career might wear him down.

Johnny Rotten, lead singer of the punk rock band the Sex Pistols, was one of the leaders of the 1970s music scene.

The last move

Blue Moves, Elton John's first album for his own label, Rocket, was released at the end of 1976. Its generally downbeat tone reflected the various crises in the lives of its two creators. Despite their established recipe for success and all their fame, Elton John and Bernie Taupin seemed to be drifting apart.

In addition, the antics of the Sex Pistols were dominating newspaper headlines. Johnny Rotten had suddenly become a much more newsworthy topic than Elton John. As the next few years showed, Elton John's lingering popularity was due mainly to old fans. He did not seem to be able to attract any new converts.

Rolling Stone

To promote the new album, a jaded Elton John gave only two interviews to the music press. One, to *Melody Maker*, brought out nothing remarkable. The other, to *Rolling Stone* magazine, turned out to be the most revealing of all Elton John's interviews.

John's sexuality had been a topic that was often speculated about in the press. Nobody ever addressed it directly, however. In this interview, *Rolling Stone* journalist Cliff Jahr edged closer to learning the answer to

Opposite: Under Elton John's management, the Watford Football Club became a champion team.

Below: As his music career declined, Elton John turned to his second childhood passion, soccer, and became chairman of the Watford Football Club.

the persistent question: "What is Elton John's sexual orientation?" The resulting article was entitled "Elton's Frank Talk: The Lonely Life of a Superstar." In it, John revealed that he was bisexual; he was attracted to both women and men. As to why he had never talked about it previously, he said, "Nobody asked me about it before." Despite some changes in attitudes during the 1970s, very few stars in the entertainment industry admitted that they were bisexual or homosexual. It was a major step for Elton John.

The number of record sales needed to sustain the lifestyle of a star of Elton John's magnitude meant that he could not afford to alienate any segment of the record-buying public. Large sectors of society disapproved of different forms of sexuality, however, and many did not support Elton John because they did not agree with his lifestyle. It was American sales that were hit hardest. "Everyone goes 'love and peace, man,'" John commented bitterly. "But it will never happen because hatred is rammed into their kids by parents—and hate makes much more money."

The *Rolling Stone* article had an immediate impact on record sales. The next two singles from *Blue Moves*, released after John's revelations, made a paltry showing in the charts.

An ailing megastar

The rest of the 1970s were the lowest point of Elton John's musical career. In November 1977, he gave a concert to aid Goaldiggers, a charity organization that provided soccer equipment for underprivileged children. It was a very emotional evening, at the end of which John made an announcement: "This is going to be the last show. There's a lot more to me than being on the road."

He wanted to devote more time to his other career as chairman of Watford Football Club. The team had a new manager who brought the club from the bottom level of the soccer league to the top rank in just five years. As club chairman, Elton John watched his musical career disintegrate as Watford began its meteoric rise. "I don't intend to miss a match, either home or away," John announced. "I've reached the stage where I don't need to chase all over the world as I used to."

An end to the duo?

Even as he worked as Watford's chairman, Elton John found time to record an album. It was perhaps the most cheerless end to this phase of his career, though. The album marked a suspension of the John-Taupin writing effort. With no tours to keep them together, the duo had drifted apart.

The vacancy left by Bernie Taupin was taken up by a jingle-writer named Gary Osborne, whose lyrics had been used to advertise a wide range of products from banks to chewing gum. The result of the new collaboration was the album *A Single Man*. The only major hit from the new album was John's moving instrumental "Song for Guy," which he dedicated to Guy Burchill, a Rocket employee who had been killed in a motorcycle crash. "There was never any question of splitting up," said Elton. "I wrote the 'Single Man' album with Gary Osborne

and Bernie had an album out with Alice Cooper so people put two and two together and said, 'They've broken
up.' But sometimes it's necessary to be apart."

Another first

Just a year later, Elton John became the first Western
rock star to be invited to cross the Iron Curtain and perform in what was then the Soviet Union. His voluntary
exile from the stage for just under a year had already
come to an end as he scheduled a number of American
and European appearances at the beginning of 1979.
The Soviet trip was no ordinary concert, however. The
fact that he was even considered for a performance in the
Communist nation confirmed John's status as a rock star.

On Sunday, May 20, 1979, John arrived in the
Soviet Union. During his tour, he played four shows. It
was later discovered that 95 percent of tickets had gone
to Communist Party officials. Even so, as the evening
progressed, Elton John fans managed to force their way
up to the front and liven up the event.

By the end of the trip, even party officials had
warmed up to "Comrade John," as he was nicknamed.
John remembered "crying his eyes out" on a train as
hundreds of children threw their best-loved possessions in the window. He recalled, "We spent ten days
there and had the most fantastic time, culturally as
well, seeing the most beautiful things."

The 1980s

The early years of the 1980s were dominated by video.
Music became soundtrack to visuals. Elton John had
made a mini-movie for his single "Ego" back in 1978,
but it had never been seen because the song never pen-
etrated the Top 30. Later on, however, he made good
use of the new video industry.

After the grubby monotony of punk and the rhyth-
mic glitter of disco, there was suddenly room for artists
as diverse as Michael Jackson, Prince, Boy George, and
Bruce Springsteen. There was certainly room for Elton
John, even if it had to be in a scaled-down version. "I
don't have to do handstands on the piano any more,"

he announced to music fans of the new decade. "I can concentrate on my music."

Releases

Despite the positive outlook of the 1980s, Elton John was about to take a dramatic step in another direction. Dick James had been the first person to believe in Reggie Dwight. James had also been there long after others had given up and moved on to more conventional musical artists. By now, however, the relationship between Elton John and his one-time mentor had deteriorated to a point where negotiations between them were strained. Elton John's manager, John Reid, came to believe that Dick James Music had been depriving Elton of his fair share of money from record sales. Doubts had risen in Reid's mind about the contracts John and Taupin had signed with Dick James Music in 1968 and 1973.

Musical contracts can last for many years. The terms that seemed fair when a newcomer signed his first contract could seem very unfair after he or she had become successful, however. John Reid definitely felt that Elton John had not been given his rightful portion of the enormous amount of money he had brought into Dick James Music from 1968 to 1976.

The record industry works in complicated ways. There are two basic components: publishers and record companies. Publishers own the rights to any perform-

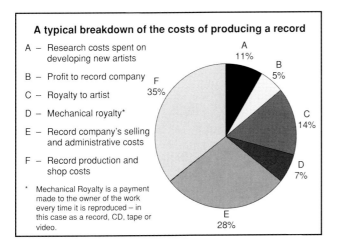

A typical breakdown of the costs of producing a record

A – Research costs spent on developing new artists

B – Profit to record company

C – Royalty to artist

D – Mechanical royalty*

E – Record company's selling and administrative costs

F – Record production and shop costs

* Mechanical Royalty is a payment made to the owner of the work every time it is reproduced – in this case as a record, CD, tape or video.

A 11%
B 5%
C 14%
D 7%
E 28%
F 35%

This pie chart shows the average costs of producing a record, CD, or tape during the 1990s. As the chart shows, artists receive only 14 percent of the money made from their work.

ance of a certain song, any broadcast of the song, publication of the lyrics, or for anyone else to record the song. These rights are called the song copyright. Publishers have to give permission and receive money for any of those uses of the song. Record copyright is owned and handled by the record company. This includes only ownership of the record itself and the right to sell the records. Today, many large record companies are also publishers. That means that an entertainer can be signed to both parts of the music industry at the same time.

Many independent publishing houses do still exist in the modern music industry, though. When an artist is signed to a publishing house, that company then usually looks for a deal with a record company for the new artist. Large record companies have branches all over the world and can issue records themselves. Small record companies need to sign additional deals with distributors to issue their records worldwide. What makes this system even more complicated is that each link in the chain of publisher, record company, and distributor deducts a percentage of a song's overall profits.

Royalties

Record companies are required by law to pay a minimum of 6.25 percent of the price of a record to the publishing company, just to use the song. This does not change, whether the artist is Elton John or a member of an unknown band. The money is then split between the publishing company and the artist. Established artists can receive as much as 85 percent of these publishing royalties. Newcomers, however, might get as little as 40 percent.

Royalties from a record deal are much more flexible, and they go directly to the artist. These range from around 5 percent of the selling price of the record to around 20 percent, depending on the artist's status. In short, if artists have written and performed the material themselves, they get money from two sources at two different rates. One comes from the record company and the record itself, and the other from the publishing company and the rights to the song.

....

"I believed that I was invincible, I believed that I could survive anything but you can't and you can't carry on thinking like that because it just cuts you off from the real world."

—Elton John

....

Getting it back

Gilbert O'Sullivan had been a highly successful singer and songwriter in the 1970s. His hits had included "Claire" and "Alone Again (Naturally)." O'Sullivan brought a lawsuit against his record company. Out of an estimated $23 million in total record sales, he had been paid only about $800,000 throughout his career.

He felt he had been cheated out of a fortune by the complicated system of payment and by poor deals signed when he was a novice. O'Sullivan won his case and received massive back payments. All the copyrights, which were the property of his publishing company, were given back to him. Shortly after this ruling, John Reid brought a similar claim against Dick James and his company, Dick James Music.

John Reid and Elton John faced reporters after a stressful legal battle against Dick James Music.

Reid charged that Elton John's record royalties had been set at an extremely low rate (less than 10 percent, or less than a quarter of the going rate for a newcomer). Reid also argued that John's overseas record royalties had been whittled away by the overseas branches of the Dick James Music empire. In addition, Reid wanted the return of all of the John-Taupin copyrights to him as manager.

Almost a decade later, the case against Dick James and Dick James Music made it to court. Dick James refuted the claim that unjust agreements had given him and his company an unfair share of the record and publishing income. James felt that he had given an unknown artist a break, had believed in him, and had invested money in his career long after other producers would have ceased to do so.

Surprising many, Elton John married sound engineer Renate Blauel on Valentine's Day in 1984.

The verdict went against Dick James Music on most of the charges. Even so, Elton John and Bernie Taupin were awarded only a tiny fraction of the damages they wanted. Both sides claimed a victory.

In the end, the action was beneficial to no one because it proved to be very expensive. The money Elton John and Bernie Taupin received barely covered legal costs.

Too low for Bernie Taupin

In 1983, seven years of partial and total estrangement between Elton John and his songwriting partner, Bernie Taupin, came to an end. The result was the album *Too Low for Zero*. It marked the beginning of the second phase of thirty-six-year-old Elton John's long career.

The songs on the album sounded relaxed and confident again. Bernie Taupin was back in top form. *Too Low for Zero* provided Elton John with his most accomplished album for a decade and brought him an entirely new generation of fans.

"I Guess That's Why They Call It the Blues" was a beautiful and poignant ballad that, despite its reserved nature, roared onto the music charts. The lyrics had that old Taupin magic:

On his honeymoon, Elton John jumped into the ocean in Saint-Tropez, France.

And I guess that's why they call it the blues.
Time on my hands could be time spent with you,
Laughing like children,
Living like lovers,
Rolling like thunder, under the covers,
And I guess that's why they call it the blues.

Renate

It was in mid-1983 that Elton John's attention was drawn in the direction of one of the sound engineers who worked on his latest album. Nobody else took much notice of her until a tiny credit appeared on the album sleeve: "Special thanks to Renate Blauel."

Blauel and John had become friendly during the recording sessions, and when John was scheduled to make his next album, he insisted that Blauel work on that one as well.

Renate Blauel was a very down-to-earth person. She lived in a modest apartment in London. She never wore flashy clothes. She was charming, witty, and entertaining. "Renate was just one of the boys, in her usual jeans and t-shirt," journalist Nina Myskow remembered.

Above: Organized by Bob Geldof, the Live Aid concert of 1985 raised money for famine relief in Ethiopia.

Right: Elton John (second from the right) joined numerous musicians and celebrities for the Live Aid concert at London's Wembley stadium.

There could have been no better partner for Elton John than Renate Blauel. To the astonishment of the world, John announced that he and Blauel were engaged to be married. The wedding was planned for Valentine's Day, February 14, 1984. Elton John was thirty-six.

One hundred guests were flown to Australia where the wedding was held. Bernie Taupin and John Reid shared the best man duties. Then, the couple moved on to a honeymoon in New Zealand. The wedding trip had been scheduled around John's concert appearances.

At this time, John's relationship with one of the British tabloid newspapers, the *Sun*, began to sour. Many tabloids had made snide references and remarks about John's bisexuality. Headlines in the *Sun* showed terrible prejudice and poked fun at John.

Live Aid

By 1985, many entertainers had begun to do what Elton John had been doing since the 1970s: performances for charity. Rock stars had discovered a social conscience, and they had begun to use their fame to raise money for people in need. Bob Geldof, once the front man of an Irish post-punk band called the Boomtown Rats, had persuaded most of rock's biggest stars to record a single to help famine relief in Ethiopia. Released late in 1984, it was called "Do They Know It's Christmas?" and it sold more than 7 million copies worldwide.

The following summer, to raise additional funds, Geldof organized a concert at London's Wembley Stadium. A simultaneous event in JFK Stadium in Philadelphia was connected by satellite. No star could be better to top the bill than rock legend Elton John.

At the end of the evening, dressed in a striped frock coat, John belted out old favorites such as "Bennie and the Jets," "Rocket Man," and, then, with George Michael, sang "Don't Go Breaking My Heart." The concerts, called Live Aid, raised more than $90 million for famine relief.

Elton John and Bob Geldof worked together to make the 1985 Live Aid concert a success.

Empty hearth

Back at home, almost as soon as Elton John and Renate Blauel had walked down the aisle, speculation began about the strength of their marriage. Some newspapers wondered aloud whether Blauel simply wanted to siphon

49

away some of Elton John's fortune. Others claimed the marriage was a way to cover up John's homosexuality.

Despite the rumors, Elton John's hectic touring schedule was not altered to give him more free time for his wife. Unlike Bernie Taupin, Blauel did not like life on the road. So, while her husband jetted around the world, Renate Blauel remained in their residence in England.

The tabloid press's snide attacks continued unabated. In reports, mention of John's marriage was always preceded by either the word "rocky" or "shaky." Even more worrisome were the constant references to John's confirmed bisexuality. Much speculation also revolved around his wife's absence during one of the most terrifying periods in the life of the rock and pop singer.

While he was on a concert tour of Australia, Elton John's famous voice began to disintegrate. In the middle of songs, it disappeared and then reappeared without warning. It quickly became obvious that this was not just a case of laryngitis. John sought the advice of a specialist, but the outcome was far from reassuring. The doctor told John that the cause of his problem might be throat cancer. A week of total silence was prescribed until complete tests could be done.

Renate Blauel explained her reluctance to fly to his bedside: "We talked about it for a long time before he went to the hospital for the tests. . . . Elton said there was no need for me to be there. We agreed we would speak on the phone every day, which we do."

The wait to see Australia's leading ear, nose, and throat surgeon was excruciating. After a thorough examination, it was revealed that John's vocal chords were covered with nodules. If these were cancerous, his larynx would have to be removed. And if that happened, Elton John would not only be unable to sing; he would never be able to speak again.

An operation was performed to remove the nodules, and it was discovered that they were benign, or noncancerous. To everyone's relief, it was announced that Elton John would make a complete recovery. For the foreseeable future, though, a talking and singing ban was imposed on the star. The temporary inconvenience was a small price to pay for what had been a frighteningly close call.

. . . .

"Everyone wants to knock me down these days. But I have now decided that I will always bounce back. . . . Now that I've got my self respect back I've given up worrying about critics."

—Elton John

. . . .

*From the start,
Elton John's marriage
to Renate Blauel
was the subject
of criticism and
speculation in
the press.*

The bombshell

On February 25, 1987, it suddenly became clear that, in
past reports, the *Sun* newspaper had been only sparring
with Elton John. The newspaper's reports had been a
warm-up for a fight that now began in earnest. Readers
of the paper on the morning of February 25 were treated
to front-page headlines that accused John of a sex scandal involving young men. All the alleged gatherings had
taken place while John was married to Renate Blauel.

A source called "Graham X" said he had supplied
young boys for these occasions. It was also alleged that
drugs had been widely available at these parties. Only one
date, April 30, 1986, was mentioned. It so happened that
on that day, Elton John had been in New York with John
Reid. There were plane tickets and witnesses to prove it.

The mysterious "Graham X" was actually a man
named Stephen Hardy. He had been paid about $3,000
for the story. "They can say I'm a fat old sod, they can
say I'm untalented, they can call me a poof [homosex-
ual]," said a defiant Elton John. "But they mustn't ever
lie about me, because then I'm going to fight. And I'm
determined to be a winner."

The next headline, "Elton's Kinky Kicks" followed
John's filing of a lawsuit in which he claimed damages
against the paper. In response, another newspaper
argued that, on April 30, John had been in New York;
the paper detailed his itinerary for the day. Despite
such evidence, however, the *Sun* continued its series
with a story entitled "Elton's pink tutu party." By the
end of the scandal, Elton John had filed seventeen law-
suits against the editor of the *Sun*.

"I've never even met Elton John"

On November 6, 1987, Stephen Hardy sold his story to
another paper. This time, however, there were substan-
tial changes in the details. As Hardy later explained, "It's
all a pack of lies. I made it all up. I only did it for the
money. . . . I've never even met Elton John."

On December 12, 1989, the headline on the first
page of the *Sun* read: "SORRY ELTON." The attacks on
Elton John cost the newspaper more than $1 million.
No one had ever received such a large sum in a case

After several personal and professional traumas, Elton John decided to revamp his image. He auctioned off some of his famous costumes and many of the belongings he had accumulated over the past twenty years.

Elton John posed with two of his old stage outfits at the Sotheby's auction.

like this before. Then again, rarely had anyone ever been hounded so viciously and for less reason. Elton John had faced up to the media giant and won.

The strain of a whole year of false allegations on John and Blauel's marriage was immense. When Blauel was not present at the fortieth birthday celebrations for her husband, it seemed that another chapter of Elton John's life was drawing to a close.

Indeed, an announcement came the next day. The couple had decided to live apart but said there was no bitterness between them. Blauel and John remained very close and still loved each other. The differences between them and between their lifestyles, however, were too great to sustain a marriage.

The Sotheby's auction

In an effort to put his life in order, Elton John decided to auction off all his unwanted possessions. "Getting rid of these things is a way of divesting," he said. "I've got to get Elton out of my life and start being a little like Reg again."

Many of the famous clothes that John had worn over the years went up for auction at Sotheby's, a famous auction house. He sold a replica of Tutankhamen's throne, jukeboxes, and art nouveau figures. He also gave up his many sets of spectacles, his antiques, and his art collection. The sale took four days and raised millions of dollars.

Way out

As the 1990s began, Elton John, now in his forties, continued the charity work to which he had devoted himself for the previous twenty years. Now, however, he had found a cause that would transcend all others.

In 1990, an American teenager named Ryan White made a huge impact on Elton John's life. Ryan suffered from hemophilia, a disease that did not allow his blood to clot in the normal way. This meant that he could bleed to death from a simple cut and needed frequent blood transfusions. It was during one of these transfusions that Ryan contracted the AIDS virus from an infected blood donor.

Ryan's school tried to ban him from classes in the mistaken belief that other children might contract AIDS from him. In response, Ryan White became a campaigner for AIDS awareness, and through his television appeals, he won the hearts of the American people. For the last two weeks of Ryan's life, Elton John was at his side. Ryan White's tragic story was the spark that ignited John's determination to crusade against ignorance and to relieve the suffering of AIDS patients.

In June 1990, John rereleased two songs, "Healing Hands" and "Sacrifice," as a single and donated the proceeds to AIDS charities. The record shot up the charts and gave Elton John his first solo number one single in the United Kingdom. More importantly, it allowed hundreds of thousands of dollars to be donated to AIDS charities. "Every single I shall release henceforth," Elton John announced, "from any album will be toward charity."

Resting

In 1991, Elton John decided that he would take a well-deserved break. He had, after all, twenty years' worth of rest to catch up on. The lifestyle into which he had drifted had begun to take its toll.

As usual, however, he broke that pledge to himself and began to organize the largest and most ambitious tour of his career. It kicked off in the summer of 1991

Ryan White, photographed here with his mother, was an AIDS sufferer whom Elton John met through his involvement with AIDS charity work.

and ended with the release of his next album the following June. Throughout the year, John continued his
tireless work for AIDS charities.

That same year, Elton John began to face up to the
many addictions that had plagued him for years.
Although there had often been hints of his problems,
this was the first time he admitted them openly.
Alcoholism, cocaine addiction, and bulimia were all
part of the price he had paid for his stardom.

At the beginning of 1991, Elton John checked into
the Parkside Lutheran Hospital in Chicago, which spe-
cializes in multiple addictions. Through a regime of
deprivation and support, he was finally able to regain
some control over his life. He also attended Alcoholics
Anonymous meetings between concert dates. The Elton
John who emerged was mentally stronger and more
physically fit than he had been in years. For a start, he
was twenty-five pounds lighter.

John finally gave up his quest for miraculous hair
growth as well. He resigned himself to wearing a wig. It
was, however, not just any wig. It was reported to have
cost more than $22,000.

With Ryan White's mother, Elton John paid his respects at Ryan's funeral in April 1990.

elton john

60-02-3-0

_____ 19 __

Pay *European Aids Charities* | $ 100,000

One Hundred Thousand

Dollars Only

elton john

⑈ 0735511⑈+ 02

Above: In 1990, Elton John pledged to donate his share of the profits from all of his future singles recordings to AIDS charities.

Right: Alcohol and drug abuse had plagued Elton John for years. During the early 1990s, he sought treatment for his addictions.

Back again

In 1992, Elton John turned forty-five. He also went back into the studio to work on his next album, *The One*. The Taupin-John magic had survived through the pain and separation of the previous year. Their music was as crisp as ever, the lyrics as powerful and meaningful. The first single to be released was "The Last Song." The song addressed the AIDS issue, and the proceeds were donated to AIDS charities. John wanted a gay man's perspective on his song, and the video was directed by Gus Van Sant. "I definitely wanted someone gay to direct this video," John said. "I don't want it to come across as mushy, but I want people who see it to be touched. If they have any bigotry or fear, this can overcome them and encourage compassion."

Next, Elton John took an unprecedented step for a pop star. He announced that he planned to set up an organization, based in Great Britain, to help AIDS charities and engage in AIDS research. It would be called the Elton John AIDS Foundation. Its objectives were to

After a year's rest, Elton John returned to the stage at age forty-five to perform songs from his new album, The One.

• •

"... if I knew what I know now I would not take a drug. If I could influence one person by saying, 'Listen, life is so good, I missed so much by taking drugs.' ... So if there's one person out there that I can help and say, 'Don't do it,' don't do it."

—Elton John

• •

promote awareness of the disease in the world and to sponsor AIDS research. With money provided by John, the foundation helped AIDS sufferers directly and gave to hospitals that worked to fight the disease. John also made it clear that he wanted to devote a large part of his budget to education both within the homosexual community and in the general population. A sister organization was also set up in the United States with similar aims. Over the years, Elton John had done charity work on a vast scale. The Elton John AIDS Foundation was his crowning achievement.

An ordinary star

By the early 1990s, Elton John had cleaned up his life, fought his addictions, and claimed that he had never been happier. "I've found someone I really love," he said. "I'm quite comfortable about being gay. I've finally resolved all of the problems I ever had. I'm really happy and optimistic for the first time ever."

In a business that creates and destroys stars with careless abandon, Elton John managed to dominate two decades of pop music—more than half of the industry's total history. Few could have coped with the media onslaught that he had endured and still had the courage to live such a high-profile lifestyle. As Elton John proclaimed himself from practically every notable stage throughout the world: "I'm still standin' better than I ever did. Lookin' like a true survivor, feelin' like a little kid. And I'm still standin' after all this time. . . ."

Throughout the 1990s and into the new millennium, Elton John continued to find success with music lovers around the world. He also became well known for his friendships with other major celebrities. One relationship, in particular, showed the world how deep John's feelings were for those he loved. In 1997, England's Princess Diana, a good friend of John's, was killed in a car accident. At the funeral, John sang a moving tribute to Diana to the tune of "Candle in the Wind." The touching incident showed that Elton John's compassionate spirit was yet another reason for his fans to admire him.

Timeline

1947   March 25: Reginald Kenneth Dwight is born in Pinner, England, to Stanley and Sheila Dwight.

1958   September: Reggie becomes a pupil at Pinner County Grammar School. He also wins a part-time scholarship to the Royal Academy of Music in London.

1962   Stanley and Sheila Dwight divorce. Shortly after, Reg takes up his first professional engagement playing the piano at the Northwood Hills Hotel near his home.

1962–1963   Reggie teams up with Stuart Brown, Geoff Dyson, and Elton Dean to form a band called Bluesology.

1965   March 5: Reggie leaves school to take a job at Mills Music Publishers in London. Bluesology, now professional, releases "Come Back, Baby," written by R. Dwight.

1967   Reggie Dwight auditions for Liberty Records. He is put in touch with lyricist Bernie Taupin.
November: Dwight-Taupin formally sign with Dick James Music.
December: Reggie Dwight changes his name to Elton John.

1968   March: The first Elton John single, "I've Been Loving You Too Long," is released.

1969   June: *Empty Sky*, Elton John's first album, is released through Dick James Music.

1970   August 25: Elton John gets his big break at the Troubadour Club in Los Angeles, California.
A second album, *Elton John*, enters the charts, finally settling at number four in the United States and number eleven in Great Britain.

1971   January: Elton John has a first hit single in the United Kingdom with "Your Song." John Reid becomes Elton John's manager.

1972   Elton John has his first number one album in the United States with *Honky Chateau*.

1973   Elton John begins the year by topping the American charts for three weeks with the single "Crocodile Rock," which earns a gold disc when it sells more than four hundred thousand copies.
January: John has to fight his own record company to release the single "Daniel." It eventually reaches number four in the United Kingdom. The album *Don't Shoot Me, I'm Only the Piano Player* is released.
October: The double album *Goodbye Yellow Brick Road* is released. It lodges itself at the top of the American charts for eight weeks.

1974   February: The single "Candle in the Wind" is released. It is a hit at number one in the United States and earns Elton John a gold disc.

1975   May: The album *Captain Fantastic and the Brown Dirt Cowboy* is released.
November: Elton John appears at Dodger Stadium in Los Angeles.

1976   Elton John becomes chairman of Watford Football Club.

1978   October: Elton John releases *A Single Man*, his first album produced without the lyrical assistance of Bernie Taupin. It performs relatively well, reaching number eight in the United Kingdom and number fifteen in the United States.

1979   May: Elton John becomes the first Western rock star to perform in the Soviet Union. He plays eight concerts in Leningrad (now St. Petersburg).

1983   Elton John and Bernie Taupin reunite on *Too Low for Zero*, John's most successful album since the 1970s. It reaches number seven in the United Kingdom and number twenty-five in the United States.

1984   February 14: Elton John marries Renate Blauel. The wedding takes place in Sydney, Australia.

1985   July: Elton John headlines Live Aid, the biggest fundraising event ever for Ethiopia famine relief.

1986   January: Elton John and Bernie Taupin win their court action against Dick James Music and are awarded back payments in royalties.

1987   January: Elton John undergoes major throat surgery in Sydney after a cancer scare.
March: John and Renate Blauel formally separate.

1988   September: Elton John has two thousand of his collected possessions auctioned off at Sotheby's auction house, London.
December: John wins his lawsuit against the *Sun* newspaper and receives more than $1 million in damages from the paper.

1990   Elton John befriends Ryan White, the American teenager suffering from AIDS.
April 7: Ryan White dies.
June 23: "Sacrifice" and "Healing Hands" are rereleased. The single becomes John's first British solo number one single. John donates the proceeds to AIDS charities.
November: The Elton John AIDS Foundation is set up to raise money to help sufferers and to fund research.

Recommended Listening

• **Background:** Jerry Lee Lewis, "Whole Lotta Shakin' Goin' On" and "Great Balls of Fire."
• **Singles by Elton John:** "Your Song," "Rocket Man," "Daniel," "Candle in the Wind," "Bennie and the Jets," "Lucy in the Sky with Diamonds," "Pinball Wizard," "Song for Guy," "Little Jeannie," "Blue Eyes," "I Guess That's Why They Call It the Blues," "I'm Still Standing," "Sacrifice."
• **Albums:** *Elton John, Tumbleweed Connection, Honky Chateau, Goodbye Yellow Brick Road, Captain Fantastic and the Brown Dirt Cowboy, Two Low for Zero, Reg Strikes Back, Sleeping with the Past.*

Glossary

AIDS: Acquired Immune Deficiency Syndrome is caused by a virus that is transmitted in the blood or semen and is usually fatal. It attacks the body's immune system, preventing it from fighting other diseases.

arranger: The person who writes orchestral or other accompanying passages of music for a record.

ballad: A song with a slow tempo, often about a romantic or serious subject.

chord: A harmonious combination of notes, usually played together or in quick succession.

chorus/refrain: This is usually made up of the best part of the melody and is repeated a number of times throughout a song. It often introduces the central theme of a song, repeating both lyrics and specific musical phrases.

copyright: The ownership of a certain song or album which can be bought and sold like other goods.

demo (demonstration): A rough recording of a song to give a record company some idea of what the finished product will be like.

gold disc: A symbolic gold disc is often presented to an artist when four hundred thousand copies of a single or one hundred thousand copies of an album have been sold.

hook: Another word for refrain; "hook" gives the idea of how this part of the song must catch the listener's attention.

key: The note upon which a scale begins.

lyrics: The words of a song.

melody: A series of musical notes that form the basis of a tune.

music publisher: A company that buys songs from composers and sells these songs to record companies.

platinum disc: A symbolic platinum disc is often presented to an artist when six hundred thousand copies of a single or three hundred thousand copies of an album have been sold.

producer: The person who oversees the sound and feel of a record.

punk: A raw, rebellious music movement that grew up in the United Kingdom during the 1970s. It was identifiable by sound and fashion. Usually it had a loud, simplistic musical technique, and punk rockers wore leather gear and safety pins and had outrageous hairstyles.

record label: An individual record company.

royalty: An agreed-upon percentage of the cost of a record that is paid to the artist by the publisher or record company every time a copy of the record is sold.

syncopated rhythm: When stress is placed on the usually weaker beat, as opposed to the stronger one, in a musical piece.

tempo: The pace at which a piece of music is played, normally in keeping with the character of the piece (i.e., a love song is usually played slowly).

Index